Cows

Julie Murray

Abdo
FARM ANIMALS
Kids

abdopublishing.com

Published by Abdo Kids, a division of ABDO, PO Box 398166, Minneapolis, Minnesota 55439.
Copyright © 2016 by Abdo Consulting Group, Inc. International copyrights reserved in all countries.
No part of this book may be reproduced in any form without written permission from the publisher.

Printed in the United States of America, North Mankato, Minnesota.

052015

092015

THIS BOOK CONTAINS
RECYCLED MATERIALS

Photo Credits: iStock, Shutterstock

Production Contributors: Teddy Borth, Jennie Forsberg, Grace Hansen

Design Contributors: Candice Keimig, Dorothy Toth

Library of Congress Control Number: 2014960331

Cataloging-in-Publication Data

Murray, Julie.

Cows / Julie Murray.

   p. cm. -- (Farm animals)

ISBN 978-1-62970-939-0

Includes index.

1. Cows--Juvenile literature.   I. Title.

636.2--dc23

                    2014960331

Table of Contents

Cows

Cows live on a farm.

Most cows are black, brown, or white. Some have spots or **markings**.

Girls are called cows.

Boys are bulls.

Babies are calves.

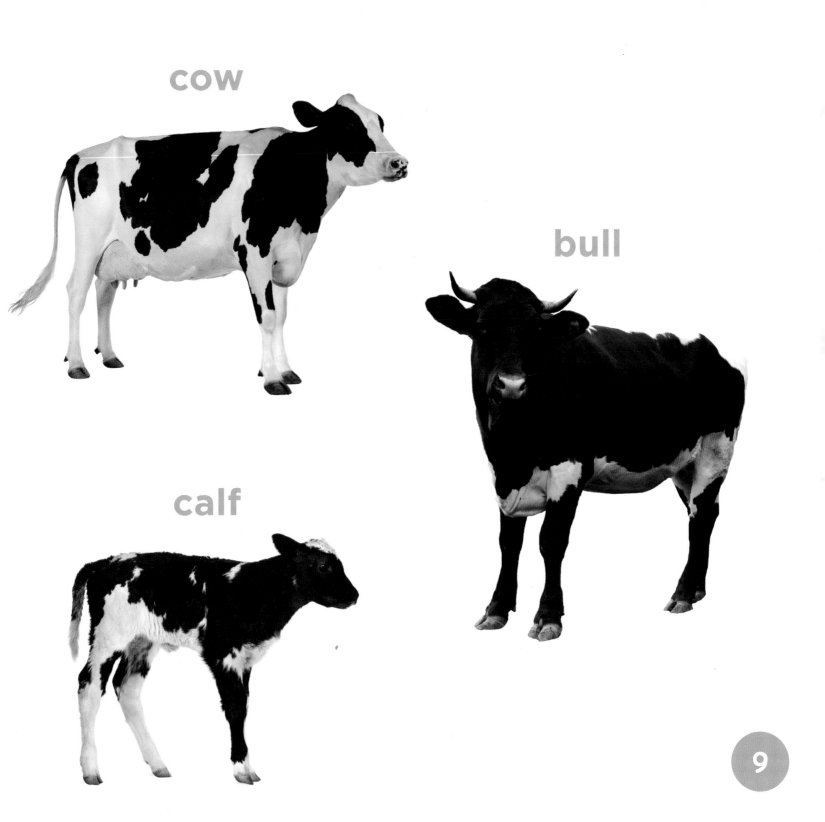

cow

bull

calf

Cows say, "moo."

Cows eat hay and grass.

They also eat **grain**.

Cows eat a lot. They eat about 50 pounds (23kg) of food a day!

People drink cow's milk.

The milk is used to make butter.

It also makes ice cream!

Have you eaten a beefsteak?

It came from a cow!

Have you seen cows on a farm?

A Cow's Life

drink water

graze

get milked

rest

Glossary

grain
the seeds of plants that are used for food.

marking
a mark or repeated mark on an animal's fur or skin.

Index

abdokids.com

Use this code to log on to abdokids.com and access crafts, games, videos, and more!

Abdo Kids Code:
FOK9390